Lindsay Taylor

A – Z Pearls of Wisdom
for Executive PAs

A – Z Pearls of Wisdom for Executive PAs

First published by Your Excellency Limited, The Lodge, Bath Place, Clifton, Bedfordshire SG17 5HE, UK. www.yourexcellency.co.uk.

Edited by Angela Garry (angelagarry@picaaurum.com)

First published 2015.

British Library Cataloguing-in-Publication Data

A catalogue entry for this book is available from the British Library.

ISBN-13: 978-1517705749

ISBN-10: 1517705746

Printed and bound by www.createspace.com

Table of Contents

Introduction and message from the author

Hello! My name's Lindsay Taylor.

I'm a former PA and now Director of Executive Coaching & Training organisation Your Excellency Limited. I specialise in delivering down-to-earth, fun and beneficial learning to PAs and Administrative Professionals. I've collated a wealth of input from professionals across the world in response to my questions "What is an Executive PA?" and "What skills and attributes are needed to be an effective and efficient Executive PA?".

I understand the diversity of the PA role - how it can differ from organisation to organisation, from sector to sector, from team to team. That's what makes the role so exciting. It's also what makes the role so challenging. More and more organisations are realising the worth of their Administrative Professionals. Executive PAs are increasingly being accepted as one of the management team – with this status comes the need for specific skills and attributes, specific pearls of wisdom - that are crucial for your overall success.

I've pulled together these pearls of wisdom in a useful A-Z format which I know Executive PAs and Administrative Professionals across the world will find not only useful and beneficial – but essential in today's demanding business environment. You can find out more about our training and development opportunities on our website at www.yourexcellency.co.uk.

I'd like to say a huge "Thank you!" to the following:

- My husband, son and daughter for their support and feedback.
- Angela Garry of Pica Aurum for invaluable self-publishing knowledge and pulling this book into the amazing format you see now.
- DeskDemon.com for featuring the original Pearls of Wisdom on their website and for providing a fantastic resource for PAs.
- Louise Lloyd for her insightful wisdom in providing the W is for Wellness Pearl.
- The Original Pearly Kings and Queens Association for providing the "Delivering Pearls of Wisdom" image for the front cover.
- Nick Fewings who provides the images to complement each Pearl of Wisdom (more of Nick's images can be viewed on his Flickr work-stream www.flickr.com/photos/jannerboy62).
- My friends across the world who have provided testimonials to endorse this book,

And, of course,

- A heartfelt thanks to you – the dedicated Executive PAs and Administrative Professionals who I have had the pleasure to train and work with.

Thank you all.

Lindsay Taylor x

A – Z Pearls of Wisdom
for Executive Pas

"I will blink before you do"　　　　　　　Few Peeps©

A is for Assertiveness

A is for...Assertiveness

We've all heard of the "fight" or "flight" syndrome - when faced with situations outside of our control our immediate reaction is likely to be one that is either:

* **Aggressive** - where we react with verbal / physical aggression, or
* **Passive** - where we run away physically or mentally (by burying our heads in the sand or ignoring it).

It's a primal response that stems way, way back.

Imagine yourself now - way, way back in time – let's say the Stone Age.

You've spent the morning kitting your cave out with the top of the range stone accessories (carved by your own fair hands) and you're looking forward to a relaxing evening watching the sunset.

So when an intruder approaches your cave (he's heard of your talent with carving stone accessories and fancies taking something for himself!) your instinctive reaction is likely to be one of two responses – do you:

a) pick up the heavy brick club that you keep by your side at all times, wave it high above your head and fight him off or

b) take flight out of the back entrance of your cave as fast as your deer-skin-clad little feet will take you (flight)?

Quite simply, in easy-cave-like-primal-terms, that's what the fight or flight response is!

In the work place the "fight / aggressive" or "flight / passive" responses are inappropriate, ineffective and with obvious negative implications to you and your team.

Neither response will win you the respect of your team members or ensure you are considered a valued professional.

Recognising when the primal fight / flight reaction could potentially take hold is crucial for your success.

Understanding that you have a choice over your reactions is paramount – as is the knowledge that the best choice available to you is "assertiveness".

What is "assertiveness"?

For me, it's about standing up for what you think, for what you believe in – and at the same time respecting the fact that not everyone will think the same as you do.

People have different perspectives - everyone "ticks" differently and we are all unique in the way we are made-up.

This is what makes the world such an exciting place to be. This is what makes the world such a challenging place to be.

How do we respond and communicate assertively?

Based on the research of former Harvard Professor Albert Mehrabian, face-to-face communication when sharing our thoughts and feelings can be broken down into three areas –

1)   the words that we speak
2)   the tone that we use and
3)   the body language that we use.

The words that we speak account for 7% importance in getting our message across, the tone for 38% and the body language for 55%.

If we use Mehrabian's research in terms of responding assertively then it is clear that we need to pay attention to *how* we deliver our assertive message as well as the actual words and verbage we use.

I am an advocate of the saying "failing to plan is planning to fail" – so where possible take time to plan your assertive response.

You can think about your response in terms of the 3 Mehrabian's areas with the following "checklists":

Assertive Words:

- Be open, honest and to the point.
- Use "I" statements – this is about your view.
- Share your feelings – take ownership of the fact that we are emotional beings.
  Say "I feel...." and claim the emotion you are feeling.
- Acknowledge your own rights, wants and needs.
- Ask questions of others to find out their wants and needs.
- Empathise with the other person's views and respect the fact that people are different and have different views.

- Focus on problem solving, moving forward and thinking about the future.
  The ideal outcome for any assertive response is for a win-win situation.
  Propose a way forward and then "bounce" this back to your recipient asking them what they think.

Assertive Tone

- Think about how you say the words.
- Speak the meaning, not just the words.
- Think about the timing of your response – put your own view forward and allow others to have their say.
- Ensure your breathing is relaxed and steady.
- Use evenly spaced words.
- Speak at an even pace.
- Emphasise key words.

Assertive Body Language

- Ensure your eye contact is direct, relaxed and gentle.
- Deliver your message at the same eye level to your recipient(s).
- Keep your posture upright and balanced ("plant" your feet firmly on the ground – so you feel truly "grounded").
- Ensure you face the other person and at the same time respect their personal space.
- Ensure your gestures are balanced and open.
- Ensure your facial expression is open and pleasant.

Assertiveness Aura

In addition I believe assertiveness is at its most powerful when you achieve an Assertiveness Aura – a state of being, a presence, an aura that comes from your belief in yourself – the belief that you are entitled to be assertive, that your opinion is valued and deserves the respect of others.

The 'A' Pearl:

> *"Say what you mean and mean what you say"*
> *Lindsay Taylor*

"Framing the Day Ahead" Few Peeps©

B is for Beliefs

B is for... Beliefs (Your Mind is Your Kingdom)

16th Century English Poet Francis Quarles famously stated ***"my mind is my kingdom"***.

If we take time to think about Quarles' meaning, in essence we are creating a rich kingdom in our own minds and ironically substantiating his claim and statement.

Interpreting Quarles' quote further, if we consider our mind to be our own kingdom we are ultimately the "King" or "Queen" of our domain. We have complete control and authority of it - we can rule our kingdom as we see fit - but do we?

Understanding the power of our own thinking and "tapping" into our mind can be highly beneficial, indeed a necessity, in being successful in our everyday lives and achieving all those things we want or need to achieve.

Hold the belief that "I am in charge of my mind and therefore my results" and understand that, crucial to our overall success is the recognition that - sometimes the way our mind operates can be unhelpful to us and - we have control over our own mind and can "reprogramme" it accordingly.

We all have "voices in our heads", internal dialogues and conversations going on in our mind.

Sometimes these voices can say some pretty unhelpful things – we can hold beliefs and thoughts that can limit or stop us from doing things. These are what we call "limiting beliefs".

Henry Ford famously said ***"If you believe you can or believe you cannot do something, either way you are likely to be right"***.

It's true – by saying you "can't" do something you are already setting yourself up to not do it!

It's important to notice when the voices in your mind are talking and then take control of these voices (as if we have a giant personal remote control in hand).

We can pause the voices, we can turn down the volume and, more importantly, we can "reprogramme" these voices.

We can reprogramme the limiting beliefs to something much more useful – we can presuppose something to be true and hold enabling beliefs that will enable us and help us to achieve things.

Enabling beliefs can be inspirational, powerful and motivational – they can help us "unlock" our thinking and be curious about a situation so we can get a different perspective.

We can hold a belief to be true in certain situations to help us and others – to enable us to move forward and achieve our objectives, goals and outcomes.

We can experiment with our own thinking and this can give us flexibility in our feelings and behaviours.

At times when we feel stuck or confused with various situations we are faced with we can hold an enabling belief.

The following are just a handful of motivational enabling beliefs, two with corresponding narrative to their potential use and others for you to think about yourself – employing the strategy that Your Mind is Your Kingdom.

"If you always do what you've always done, you will always get what you've always got"

If something isn't working and you are doing the "same old thing" over and over again you will get the same result.

By doing something differently it might give you a different (and maybe better) result.

By seizing an opportunity to try things in a different way you are opening up all sorts of possibilities – and if you don't try things in a different way, how will you know what you are missing out on?

This is where knowledge sharing and networking comes into greatest effect.

You can learn from other administrative professionals by sharing knowledge and best practice.

In the interactive world of the world wide web, there are some amazing resources out there – all available at the touch of a button on your laptop or trusty "hand held". My daughter's favourite saying is "if you don't know something, Google it, mummy!"

Build up your own Resources List for inspirational sources of information and a catalyst for putting into practice this enabling belief.

"There is no such thing as failure, only feedback"

Many of you will have a formal appraisal process at your organisations. Recognise that feedback is crucial to your overall success and high quality feedback is given for your own career progression.

Those voices in our head may receive certain feedback with a response along the lines of "well, you failed there didn't you!". Sound familiar? This is not a particularly useful internal dialogue to have.

By holding the belief that "there is no such thing as failure, only feedback" will open up more opportunities and possibilities for you to learn from feedback.

So, the project you've worked on may not have gone as well as you liked or hoped – so what can you learn from it?

Knowing what you now know, in hindsight, what could you have done differently?

If you were to run a similar project again, what could you do more of? Less of?

What will you replicate? What will you do the same? What will you do differently?

And here are some other enabling beliefs for you to think about - remembering that Your Mind Is Your Kingdom...

- "Choice is better than no choice."
- "If one person can do something then anyone can."
- "The person with the most flexibility in thinking and behaviour has the most influence over any interaction."
- "I am in charge of my mind and therefore my results."

The 'B' Pearl:

> *"The happiness of your life depends on the quality of your thoughts"*
> *Marcus Aurelius*

"Synchronised Fish and Chip Eating"   Few Peeps©

C is for Communication

C is for... Communication

As an Executive PA you need to communicate with internal and external customers. Very quickly you need to get on someone else's wavelength in order to communicate effectively with them and create good rapport. You need to think about the best way to communicate in any given situation (face to face, email, text message, telephone call...) then think about the language you will use to communicate.

People use terminology, phrases and words that relates to how they process their world and that's what I want to introduce in this Pearl of Wisdom.

We are all complex beings - with neurological pathways buzzing with activity, skilfully multi-tasking with organisational expertise and company knowledge at our fingertips... we are seeing, hearing, feeling, smelling and tasting our way to PA excellence and success!

But did you know that, whilst we access all five senses to "make sense" of our worlds, in fact most of us have a dominant or primary sense that we use over the others? That dominant sense can mean we favour certain words, phrases and vocabulary.

Being able to identify your own and others dominant sense can be a useful thing to do to ensure you communicate as effectively as possible.

Take a few minutes to think back to the last meeting you were involved in and re-live the most memorable bits - collect the memories in your mind.

Then, think about how you remembered: Did you create a visual picture of the events? Was it a "snapshot", a still image? Was it a "mini movie"? Was it in colour?

Or did you notice the sounds within the experience - people's voices, music or the natural sounds of the surroundings?

Or maybe the memory was about feelings inside - happiness (the meeting went really well!) or tension (the Sales Director and Managing Director could not agree on anything!).

Whichever one of these ways of reconstructing your memory was the first and / or most recognisable indicates your likely dominant sense - or your lead Representational System. Quite simply, it is how you create a "representation" or "re-present" your world - either in

- pictures (the Visuals - or The V)
- sounds (the Auditory - or The A)
- or feelings (the Kinaesthetics - or The K).

This is our VAK System - one that you as a PA can tap into to communicate really effectively with the people you work with.

An indicator of your Representation or VAK System is the language that you use - particular words and phrases that we call "Predicates".

The V

If you have a predominantly Visual Representational System then you're likely to use words and phrases like:

- "I see what you mean."
- "I get the picture"
- "Things are looking great."
- "We need to focus on this aspect."

and, because you can see in your "mind's eye" what you're talking about you're likely to use your arms and body to draw out in front of you the very thing you're describing! You will notice how things look around you - their shape, form and colour - the aesthetics.

The A

If you have a predominantly Auditory Representational System then you're likely to talk in predicates that are sound or music related, as examples then

- "We discussed the situation"
- "I'd like to listen to your ideas"
- "I do like the sound of that".

You might be great at tuning into new ideas.

The K

If you have a predominantly Kinaesthetic Representational System then you're likely to use language that is feelings, movement or touch related:

- "I'm under pressure"
- "I like the feeling of that"
- "Things are really moving now"
- "He's hot on quality control"

You probably have a pretty clear idea of where you experience your feelings too. If you're stressed you may touch your head, if you're hungry you may touch your stomach and for you to really optimise any learning, you probably want to be there, doing it as a first-hand experience.

So, why is this useful I hear you cry? "Tell me more" say the Auditory readers!

"I get a feeling this is really beneficial stuff - how can I take this great new learning and really get to grips with it in the office to communicate effectively?" ask the Kinaesthetic readers.

"So, that's great you've painted a picture of what this VAK thing is all about – can we look at it in relation to the Executive PA role?" you Visual readers request.

What is the use of my newfound knowledge?

Before I answer your question, let me ask you a couple of questions.

How often have you met someone for the first time and felt that you got along really well and immediately seemed to be on the "same wavelength"? And...How often have you met someone for the first time and found it really difficult to keep the conversation going?

The reason for this could be because you are either talking the same or a different "VAK Language".

If a primarily visual person is using all their visual type predicates, an auditory person is likely to "switch off". However two "visual" people are much more likely to create quicker and deeper rapport and be "comfortable" with each other because they are, in effect, talking the same language.

So, next time you are listening to colleagues or friends in conversation, notice what words they tend to use and favour. Read through your emails in your inbox and notice any patterns of predicates favoured by those you work with. What Representational System do you think they are?

If you've discovered you are a primarily Visual Representation System and your manager is Auditory - in order to communicate effectively with him / her you can adjust your language and include more auditory predicates.

And that just leaves me to end this Pearl of Wisdom with a beautiful quote from Nelson Mandela who said "If you talk to a man in a language he understands, that goes to his head. If you talk to him in his language, that goes to his heart".

The 'C' Pearl:

> *"If you speak to a man in a*
> *language he understands,*
> *that goes to his head.*
> *If you speak to him in his*
> *language that goes to his*
> *heart"*
> *Nelson Mandela*

"The Piggyback of True Love"   Few Peeps©

D is for Delegation

D is for...Delegation

Rarely does Delegation take the limelight – the starring role as an important "technique" for your overall success (and the overall success of your team). So in this Pearl of Wisdom (drum-roll please), I'd like to welcome to the stage: Delegation.

I've called Delegation a "technique". In my opinion, that is what it is and, as with any technique it takes practice. Let's think about Delegation in terms of the following:

- What are the reasons people don't delegate?
- What's important about delegating?
- The "when" of delegation
- The "who" of delegation
- The "how" of delegation

What are the reasons people don't delegate?

So, I put my hand up….here I am sharing my wisdom on delegation and I own up to the fact that, in the past, I haven't delegated because that little voice in my head is saying "I like doing things my way. I know how to do this – so it's easy just to do it myself rather than to take the time and effort to explain it all to someone else. Anyway they might not do it the same way as me – and, of course, my way is the best".

Sound familiar?! We need to understand that delegation is important.

So, what's important about delegation?

1. You can free up your time to develop skills in other areas
2. You can develop other people's skills and abilities

So, there's another D word that skips hand-in-hand across the stage with Delegation.

Development

In essence, delegation allows you to make the best use of your time and skills and it helps other people in the team grow and develop to reach their full potential.

The "When" of Delegation

The power of questioning comes into being here! Ask yourself:

Is this a task that only I can do – or can someone else do it?

Does the task provide an opportunity to grow and develop another person's skills?

Is this a recurring task?

By delegating now, will I be saving time in the long term?

Do I have enough time to delegate the task effectively?

You need to think about the time involved in any training provision, questions and answers, opportunities to check progress and rework if necessary.

Keep thinking long-term. This might take some time and effort now. However in the long-term you could be freeing up your time and ultimately aiding development.

The "Who" of Delegation

Think about the person you are delegating to.

What skills, knowledge and experience do they have in relation to the task?

Are they going to need training (and do you have the time and resources available to provide this)?

What do you know about the way this person likes to work?

How independent are they?

What do they want from their job?

What is their current workload like and do they have time to take on more work?

The "How" of Delegation

Firstly, as with any situation, you need to be really clear about your desired outcome – what is it you want or need to achieve?

Involve the person in the whole delegation process – discuss and decide with them what tasks are to be delegated.

Agree with them how this will work.

Should the person wait to be told what to do? Ask what to do? Recommend what should be done then act? Act and then report results immediately? Take action then report periodically?

Ensure you match responsibility with authority (remembering that ultimate accountability is with you).

Communication flow is key and you need to be available to answer questions.

Quieten that little voice in your head that says your way of completing a task is the best – someone else may complete the task differently to you.

We all have our own ways of working. Ensure you focus on the result.

Get the person to recommend solutions and problems (rather than simply providing the answer) and ensure you provide praise and recognition throughout.

Discuss timelines and deadlines and set aside time to review submitted work.

Get the balance right between giving enough space for people to use their abilities whilst still monitoring and supporting them to ensure the job is done effectively.

Only accept work you are satisfied with – if you accept work you are not satisfied with the team member will not learn to do a task properly.

Share the Belief that ***"There is no failure, only feedback"*** and that the best feedback is given for someone's development.

So, there we are. Delegation and Development have taken the limelight – our stars of the stage and I'm sure you'll join me in giving them the standing ovation they deserve.

The 'D' Pearl:

"One of life's greatest joys comes not from what you achieve in your life, it's what you inspire others to achieve in theirs"

Nick Fewings

"A Mother's Touch"   Few Peeps©

E is for Empathy

E is for... Empathy

Empathy (according to www.diffen.com) is *"the ability to mutually experience the thoughts, emotions, and direct experience of others"*.

A useful thing to be able to do I'm sure you'd agree, particularly in your position as an Executive PA working with lots of different characters.

So what is the benefit of being empathetic and how can we best empathise with our managers and teams?

What is the benefit of being empathetic?

By empathising with someone, you are taking the time and effort to try to understand things from their point of view.

You are working with the fact that most of us like to be (and indeed want to be) valued and respected in the workplace.

We want people to take the time to understand things from our point of view.

By empathising with someone you are gaining more of an awareness of a situation – and that can open up choice, opportunities and flexibility around your own behaviours.

By empathising with someone and respecting and valuing them – they, in turn will respect and value you. And that sets a pretty solid foundation for a great working relationship, I'm sure you'd agree.

How can we best empathise with our managers and teams?

When empathising face to face with our managers and teams, use the research of former Harvard Professor Albert Mehrabian. As a reminder from the A is for Assertiveness Pearl of Wisdom "communication can be broken down into three areas –

1)   the words that we speak
2)   the tone that we use and
3)   the body language that we use".

To empathise with someone match their words, tone and body language – by taking on the physiology of someone else you will more easily be able to identify with what they are experiencing.

Think about what you already know about the person you want to empathise with. What's important to them? See, hear and feel the world from their perspective.

Put the person you are empathising with at the forefront of the conversation. Be precise in the language that you use. Say things like:

- "I appreciate your point of view and… "
- "I can see / hear where you're coming from and… "
- "I get your perspective and… "
- "It's obvious to me that you're really passionate / upset / frustrated / excited with this… "
- "I understand how you are feeling… "

Sound back and repeat particular words or phrases that they have used. A person's vocabulary, the terms and words they use are "precious" to them – they mean something to them (which could be different to your own interpretation).

Keep gentle eye contact. Let the person finish saying what they want to say. Regular nods of your head will indicate you are listening and value what they are sharing with you.

And then, ask that one Great Question - "what do you need from me?".

The 'E' Pearl:

> *"The great gift of human beings is that we have the power of empathy"*
> Meryl Streep

"I will"   Few Peeps©

F is for Feedback

F is for... Feedback-to-self & Focus (not Flibbertigibbet)

I really do like the sound of that word: Flibbertigibbet.

It's eccentric and flighty and has an onomatopoeic quality.

However, I most certainly do not like it when I become that word - a flibbertigibbet flitting from one thing to the next, a bit of this, a bit of that (without completing or achieving anything in full!).

I know when it happens too... .when my "to do" list extends to more than one A4 page, when my inbox is full of unopened and unread messages, when I have deadlines to meet, when I glance at my watch and see that I'm "running out of time"... then.

My flitting, scatter-brained and unfocused flibbertigibbet self is far from productive.

For me, this is a prime "Feedback –to-Self and Focus" moment.

My first bit of Feedback to Self is "well done"! Well done for recognising that this is what is happening (and for being honest with myself!). Having awareness of what's going on in a situation – what's happening for you – is a Great Thing. Because once you have awareness you can then take ownership of the situation and you have choice and opportunity available to you to change the situation (for the better of course!). So with awareness comes opportunity. And with opportunity comes change.

A great model to use for Feedback-to-Self and Focus is the ABC model, the basis of which lies in asking great questions of yourself (and answering them honestly!)

A - Antagonist

What specifically is it that has happened to make me behave this way?

What can I do to eliminate or change this Antagonist in the future?

(and remember that belief "if you can't change something, change the way you think about it"!)

B – Behaviour

What behaviour am I exhibiting?

How helpful is this behaviour?

What could I be doing more of?

What could I be focusing more on?

What could I be doing less of?

What could I be focusing less on?

What could I stop doing?

What could I stop focusing on?

What could I start doing?

What could I start focusing on?

What could I continue doing?

What could I continue focusing on?

What have I done in the past that has worked in a similar situation?

What have I focused on in the past that has worked in a similar situation?

What resources do I have available to me?

What do I need to Focus on that is Urgent?

What do I need to Focus on that is Important? (Thank you Stephen Covey!)

What do I need right now?

C – Consequence

What is it I want (or need) to achieve?

What is the consequence of my current behaviour?

How useful is this consequence?

What would a better consequence be?

What do I want (or need) the consequence to be?

The 'F' Pearl:

> *"If we did all the things we are capable of, we would literally astound ourselves"*
> *Thomas Edison*

"Checking you're on the list"   Few Peeps©

G is for Gatekeeper

G is for...Gatekeeper

As a PA and Administrative Professional, what other titles can you relate to?

Gate Keeper, Tea maker,

Peace Maker, Juggler,

Mind Mapper, Networker,

Time keeper, Trainer.

Fortune Teller, Lion Tamer,

Dictionary, Thesaurus,

Mind Reader, Zoo Keeper

Mentor, Minute Taker.

Proof Reader, Typist,

Coach, Decision Maker,

Trouble-shooter, Acrobat,

Superhero, Negotiator

Right Hand, Left Hand,

Team Motivator,

Travel Booker, Budgeter,

Events Co-ordinator.

The 'G' Pearl:

> *"What you allow is what will continue"* **Anonymous**

"All because he doesn't want wet feet"

Few Peeps©

H is for Helpful

H is for... Helpful

When I ask my clients for a skill and attribute beginning with "H", "Helpful" always appears top of the list and that's understandable. It's understandable because the very nature of the role of an Executive PA is one of assisting and helping others out to ensure the manager(s), office and organisation are operating as smoothly as possible.

I know. I've been there. As a former EA working for a team of attorneys in a busy legal department in the US, I was "helpful" personified. I also kept an objective view that being helpful doesn't necessarily mean we say "yes" all the time.

We are not being helpful to ourselves, our sanity and wellbeing if we always say "yes". We need to be really clear about where our work priorities lie – what the boundaries of our role are in order that we concentrate our time and energy on the right things. It's okay to say "no" and that, in itself, is an art form.

Helpful ways to say "no" (without actually saying the word "no"!)

Use the "no" that fits best with your situation. As general guidance, remember someone has probably asked you to help them because they believe you are capable and able to do it. Thank them for asking you. Help the other person understand your point of view and perspective by saying "I'm sure you will appreciate… ".

1. The "Final Word" no

"Thank you for asking me. I would prefer not to do this. As I'm sure you will appreciate I have a deadline to meet for preparation of the management meeting packs"

2. The Rescheduling No

"Whilst I can't do it now - I could certainly help you later".

Make sure you keep your promise to the person you have agreed to help out. Make a diary note or set a reminder. This will maintain your credibility and professionalism in the workplace.

3. The Problem Solving No

"I'm not in a position to help you, have you considered phoning technical support?"

Suggest an alternative solution to the person asking for your help. We've all worked for the manager who states "Come to me with solutions, not problems" and this "no" satisfies this practice.

4. The Negotiating No

"If I help you with x, then I would really appreciate your help with y. Is that okay?"

Get the others person's agreement to this negotiation. This is a great opportunity to help each other out by tapping in to each other's expertise, skills and love for doing a particular aspect of work.

5. The Reprioritising No

"I'm happy to do this, however I'll have to reprioritise my workload a bit. What would you suggest?"

6. The "One Last Time" No

"I know I've helped you in the past and I'll help you again this time. As I'm sure you will appreciate, with my demanding workload my priorities need to be with xxxxx so from now on could I suggest you ask technical support / follow the printed procedures I've produced. Is that okay?"

Get the other person's agreement to this suggestion. In some situations you can produce an "operators manual" or typed instructions / procedures that can easily be followed without interrupting your time and which will ensure the other person can do this themselves ongoing.

The 'H' Pearl:

***"Be a fence jumper
instead of a fence sitter"
Robert V Taylor***

"Kayaking at low tide"

Few Peeps©

I is for Imagination

I is for... Imagination

"Your imagination is your preview to life's coming attractions" Albert Einstein.

As many of you know, I'm a Practitioner of NLP - Neuro Linguistic Programming - and share learning with an emphasis on our ability to think differently and act differently to make a difference to our lives.

Our company name, Your Excellency, really sums up what we are about – the training, coaching and personal development programmes that we provide are about you being excellent at whatever you need or want to do or be. It's all about Your Excellency.

The quote on our logo **"my mind is my kingdom"** comes from a 16th Century Poet Francis Quarles – you are ultimately "queen" or "king" of your own thinking.

Understanding the power of your own thinking and "tapping" into your own mind can be highly beneficial, indeed a necessity, in being excellent in your life and achieving all the things you want or need to achieve.

"Memory and imagination have the same neurological circuits, they potentially have the same impact".

When you imagine something, you are creating "a future memory".

This is something that you can work towards – a reference point.

A great colleague once told me that "energy flows where the attention goes". Very simply, you are more likely to achieve the very thing you are imagining.

An example of putting this power of imagination in to practice is when implementing the "Well Formed Outcomes" model to ensure you can, and will, achieve your outcomes, goals and objectives.

The Well Formed Outcome Model

Successful outcome thinking is based on establishing what you really DO WANT. If you listen to people you will often hear them talking about what they don't want. "I don't want to be overweight". "I don't want to have a holiday in rainy England anymore."

This type of thinking is called "away from" thinking. When we make these "don't want" statements our mind creates a representation of the very thing we do not want.

Similarly, by thinking about what we do want our mind will create a representation and start to recognise it.

This type of thinking is called "towards thinking" – establishing what you "do want" enables us to be motivated, clear and precise and it can give us a sense of direction or movement.

Every day we create goals and objectives for ourselves. Sometimes these are things just to get us through the day such as being on time or working through our "to do" list. Sometimes our goals and objectives are of a much more strategic nature and are aimed at creating longer term ambitions or even fulfilling dreams.

We may have been taught to create SMART goals - Specific, Measurable, Achievable, Realistic and Time-bound.

The Well Formed Outcome technique enables you to make your everyday and strategic outcomes even SMARTer. By using your senses to design your outcomes you can ensure they become truly motivational and Well Formed.

The process in simple terms is a checklist allowing you to test and adjust your outcome through a series of self-questioning.

- **_Is the outcome stated in the positive?_**

  The outcome must be expressed in "towards" language, not "away from", e.g. the person that does not want to be overweight would turn their "away from" statement to a "towards" statement "I want to weigh 12 stones by Christmas 2018".

- **_Is it self-initiated, maintained and within my control?_**

  The outcome must be up to you. Does the outcome rely solely on you or are others going to influence actions and events which you have no control over? If so, then your outcome may need adjusting accordingly.

- **_Is it sensory specific? (see, hear, feel it)_**

  This involves imagining yourself with your outcome complete at some future point. Project yourself forward and act as if it has already happened.

Notice what you can see, notice what you hear yourself and others saying and notice how you feel.

This gives your mind a reference point of what you want to achieve. If you can see, hear and feel it and everything is congruent then your projected outcome is right for you.

- ### *What is the context?*

These are the specifics around your outcome with regard to what, where, when and with whom.

Set some realistic frames around what you are aiming for. Is it work, home and/or life in general?

- ### *How does it fit?*

How does this outcome fit with your whole life? What is the effect on other people's lives? Is this acceptable to you? What other ecologies are created? By achieving this outcome what else do you lose or disrupt?

This is known as "secondary gain" – what you get by keeping yourself in your current position.

You therefore need to determine where the greater benefits lie – in your current position or by achieving your new Well Formed Outcome.

- ### *What internal and external resources are required?*

These may be skills, time, internal states (e.g. confident, relaxed, energised, open-minded) or other people's support, remembering that they need to be within your control and self-maintainable.

- ### *What is the desirability now?*

Based on the previous checklists and feedback and adjustments required, do you absolutely still want this outcome?

- ### *What is the first step?*

So, you are ready to do it. What specifically will you do within the next 24 – 48 hours to start to move towards your Well Formed Outcome?

Well Formed Outcomes

The 'I' Pearl:

> **"If you can dream it, you can do it"**
> **Walt Disney**

"In the heat of the moment"   Few Peeps©

J is for Juggling

J is for... Juggling the demands of more than one boss

Many PAs are in roles where they are supporting more than one boss, having to juggle their time efficiently and effectively and remain calm under pressure.

The key to successful management of the demands of more than one boss comes down to great communication - with those you are supporting and with yourself!

Here is a list of useful techniques to help you successfully work with multiple bosses:

- Speak to each of your bosses individually to ensure they are aware of your workload and the fact that you are assisting other people.

  At the same time, assure them that you appreciate that their demands are important.

  Share with them the fact that you want to be as effective and efficient as possible.

  Ultimately you are all working towards the same goal of a smooth working relationship.

- Become familiar with the preferred workings of each boss - people work and 'tick' in different ways, and each boss may have different expectations of you.

You know which boss is happy with you typing up a report and circulating it without them even looking over it for final approval.

Likewise, you know the boss who will want to tweak that report (for the fifth time!) before it gets circulated.

- Verbally repeat your boss's demands to them to ensure you have understood their request correctly.

Never assume anything!

- Always ensure you know the deadline for a task, project or request so you can prioritise tasks and demands accordingly.

In theory, it's great to have a prioritised work list for the day (or week) ahead.

However, in practice, we know that this list will constantly change - just as you've just put together a prioritised list one of your bosses will appear with a mini-emergency that needs your assistance!

You need to be able to re-jig the list and be flexible in your approach.

- If you are lucky enough to have others who can help you in the office, delegate some of your workload.

For more on delegation read the D is for Delegation Pearl of Wisdom.

- When you have completed a project or demand, ask your boss for feedback.

  What would they have done differently?

  More of?

  Less of?

  Remember that good feedback is given to help your personal development and you have a choice what to do with this feedback!

- If a project or task didn't quite live up to your expectations, hold the belief that **'there is no failure, only feedback'**.

  Ask yourself: 'what would I have done differently knowing what I know now?'

  And 'how can I learn from this experience for the future?'

- Remember: you are one person with two hands - there is a limit to the tasks that you can fit into a working day.

  Be realistic with your own expectations for working your way through that prioritised list.

  Be prepared to say 'no' if you can't meet a demand or request - saying 'no' and providing alternative suggestions is a skill in its own right.

  You can read more about the different ways to say "no" in the H is for Helpful Pearl of Wisdom.

- Take inspiration from Mary Poppins! While watching this all-time classic film with my daughter I took inspiration from Mary Poppins, before she burst into song:

'In every job that must be done,

There is an element of fun.

You find the fun, and snap!

The job's a game.

And every task you undertake

Becomes a piece of cake,

A lark, a spree,

It's very clear to see

That a spoonful of sugar helps the medicine go down.'

Hold the thought that, if you approach a task or demand in the right frame of mind, with a 'spoonful of sugar' then it can become 'a piece of cake'!

There is a great saying by Henry Ford that:

'if you believe you can or believe you cannot do something, either way you are likely to be right'.

Approach all tasks in a 'can do' mind-set and you are well on the way to achieving great things and being able to juggle those demands.

The 'J' Pearl:

> **"Our success is not just defined by what we know.**
> **More importantly it is down to the strength of the relationships we build with others"**
> **Nick Fewings**

"Two stop or not two stop, that is the question" Few Peeps©

K is for KISS

K is for... KISS

KISS is an acronym for Keep It Short & Simple.

This is an effective strategy that can be used to ensure the best impact when communicating.

We all have different amounts of information that we like to process and work with.

Some people like lots of detail.

Their sentence structure is long and contains lots of "ands" – and just when you think they've finished talking and telling you what they want to say... they will add something else!

They relish having to scroll down on an email and pick up on the detail.

Other people are more "big picture".

They just want to work with a general overview or aim and don't want to get caught up in the "nitty gritty" details. Their sentence structure is shorter (and could give the impression that they are being curt or rude).

Put a detail person and big picture person together and this is when it gets interesting.

The detail individual will be craving more detail from the big picture individual.

The big picture individual may "switch off" (ever noticed someone's eyes glazing over?!) as the detail person shares too much detail with them.

The big picture individual may well miss crucial information or requests of them in their glazed over state!

As a strategy then, it is good practice to seal things with a KISS. Keep It Short and Simple.

Say what you want to say in one succinct, impactful sentence so you engage your entire audience – big picture and detail alike.

When writing emails requesting information or a response:

Ensure the request is put at the beginning of the email (so the big picture preference is more likely to read it).

Then you can back up your email with "and for those who would like more detail… " to satisfy the detail preference who wants to scroll down!

And of course, in your busy world as an Executive PA and Office Professional you will also be saving yourself valuable time and energy by using KISS.

The 'K' Pearl:

> **"If you can't explain it to a six year old, you don't understand it yourself"**
> **Albert Einstein**

"O yay, o yay, o yay"

Few Peeps©

L is for Listening

L is for... Listening with your whole body

Listening is the key to creating and maintaining rapport and the great working relationship that we all want with our manager and team.

Listening is a skill and for many of us, it is a skill we can improve on.

The crème de la crème of listening involves listening with your whole body and then mirroring or matching the person we are listening to in order to create and maintain rapport, based on the popular saying that "people like people who are like themselves".

Once we have great rapport with someone we are then more easily able to influence or persuade them – with integrity of course – so that we can achieve our goals and outcomes. The "integrity" element here is of utmost importance when influencing – we need to ensure the person we are influencing is being taken to a good place as well as ourselves in achieving our goals and outcomes.

Let's use Mehrabian's research introduced in the "A is for Assertiveness" Pearl of Wisdom as a basis for putting this "whole body listening" into practice.

"Based on the research of former Harvard Professor Albert Mehrabian, communication can be broken down into three areas –

    1)   the words that we speak

2)   the tone that we use and

3)   the body language that we use.

The words that we speak account for 7% importance in getting our message across, the tone for 38% and the body language for 55%".

Listen with your ears to the Words:

We all have a preference for phrases, terminology and favourite sayings. Our own personal interpretation of vocabulary may be very different to someone else's.

Notice what specific words and phrases the person you are listening to has used. Pick out particular phrases and words to repeat back when talking to them.

Based on the popular saying "people like people who are like themselves", by using the same "language" and words as the person you are listening to this demonstrates your respect for what they are saying.

You are keeping the conversation "clean" by using their language without "dirtying" the conversation with your own preferences. This accounts for a lot in creating and maintaining great rapport.

Listen with your ears to the Tone:

Listen to how someone is using their voice. What tone of voice are they using? What emphasis are they placing on words with the intonation of their voice? How fast or slow are they speaking? What volume are they using? What does this tell you?

Listen with your eyes to the Body Language

Based on Mehrabian's research we know that 55% of communication comes down to body language – so how we deliver our message. As a listener then we can assess a lot from noticing what is happening in a person's body language including their physiology (facial expressions), gestures and movement. What can you see happening? We can listen with our eyes and use this information to be curious about what is going on for that person.

The 'L' Pearl:

> *"The word 'listen' contains the same letters as the word 'silent'"*
> *Alfred Brendel*

M is for 'Me Time'

"Lazing on a sunny afternoon"

Few Peeps©

M is for... 'Me time'

I invite you to step into my world.

I'm co-Director of Your Excellency, a training and coaching organisation that I run with my husband Malcolm.

I'm a coach and a trainer specialising in sharing skills with PAs and Admin professionals and I travel all over the world doing it.

I'm a wife . I'm a mum. I'm a daughter. I'm a sister......that (and much more) makes up "me".

When my husband and I set up Your Excellency, we decided that we wanted to get our work/life balance right – we wanted to combine and fit our work around the children and have time to really enjoy family time and them growing up. This means that we have a lot of flexibility and choice around how we work and enjoy life - and how we spend our time.

Unfortunately in my busy life looking after the business, looking after my family – indeed looking after life itself - I omitted time to look after "me".

The balance therefore for me personally went askew. In April 2013 my health took a plummet. I spiralled down into my first ever experience of depression and I took "time out" as essential "me time" to maintain my equilibrium.

I openly and honestly share this with you as I believe the stigma attached to depression as a taboo subject needs to be dispelled. We need to be more open and share our stories to raise awareness of this indiscriminate illness.

Many in our society who have little awareness or experience of depression need to be educated when they naively ask "what do you have to be depressed about?".

What I've discovered is that the more I am open and honest, the more I share my experience with people, the more others open up to me with their own stories. And, whilst these stories are all very personal to the individual, the one resounding message and greatest learning is that "me time" is not only important but essential.

Some of you may be saying – that's all well and good but I don't have time in my busy schedule to make sure I have "me time". The key here is that we all have the same amount of time available and we all have a choice as to how to best use this time.

So, how do you ensure that "Me time" features in your life?

I'd like you to imagine that your life is a pie.

If you could divide that pie up into slices to represent your life now, what would those slices be? How big would each slice be?

Which slice or slices (if any) represent "me time"? Draw your pie on a piece of paper.

Now think about how you want your pie to be – this time ensuring you include in "me time". Draw your "want pie", dividing it up into slices. Think about what makes up quality "Me time" for you – think about when you are at your happiest.

Looking at and considering your "now pie" and "want pie" drawings, what are the differences? How can you move from the "now pie" to the "want pie"? What needs to happen? What are your first steps to take?

And remember, this is not a "one time" only exercise – thinking about your work/life balance and the inclusion of "Me time" needs to be a continuous consideration as I have personally learned.

The 'M' Pearl:

> **"It's not selfish to love yourself, take care of yourself and to make your happiness a priority.**
> **It's necessary"**
> **Anonymous**

N is for Neuro Linguistic Programming

"Contemplating life "

Few Peeps©

N is for... Neuro Linguistic Programming

Many of you know that I specialise in delivering training and coaching to PAs and Administrative Professionals across the world and that I am a former PA myself.

What you may not know is that I am a Practitioner in NLP – Neuro Linguistic Programming - and I'd love to share with you a bit more about this fascinating subject.....

Admittedly Neuro Linguistic Programming sounds very "jargonny" doesn't it?

Its abbreviation NLP looks a bit more friendly – but many of you may still be outwardly cringing and frowning whilst reading this – *"urgh – sounds complicated to me…should I carry on reading this section of the book?"* Please do

"Complicated" was in fact my reaction when I first heard of NLP some 7 years ago - but I was curious (which interestingly enough is the very foundation to all NLP learning).

NLP seemed to be popping up in conversation everywhere and I wanted to know what all the hype was about.

The more I found out, the more I became interested – so much so that I trained to be a Practitioner in NLP.

I now run a one day workshop "Be a PA with PA – Perfect Awareness" using NLP as a foundation of beneficial learning for the PA and Administrative Professional.

Where did NLP start?

NLP was born in the 1970s at the University of Santa Cruz, California.

Richard Bandler, an Information Sciences student and Dr John Grinder, a Professor of Linguistics, studied people they considered to be excellent communicators and agents of change.

From these early days NLP has developed around the modelling of excellence and understanding *"the difference that makes the difference"*.

The tools and techniques have been refined into simple, user-friendly formats that can be applied to everyday life.

The main principles are around understanding behaviour patterns of ourselves and others thereby developing flexibility in order to achieve what we really want.

Nowadays NLP is widely used by leading edge businesses to develop competitive advantage and manage change.

Additionally individuals are utilising NLP techniques for personal development inside and outside of their work environment.

Whilst training to be an NLP Practitioner I thought *"wow – if only I'd had some of these skills and awareness during my working life as a PA because this NLP stuff is really good and so relevant to the admin professional who is working with different (and sometimes hard to understand!) personalities".*

What is it?

There are lots of definitions of NLP – here are a few:

- "The art and science of personal excellence"
- "The study of subjective experience"
- "It's what makes you and other people tick"
- "A toolkit for personal and organisational change"
- "Influencing others with integrity"
- "Helping people make sense of their reality."

My personal favourite is *"It's what makes you and other people tick"* because this is a jargon-free easy-to-understand definition that really sums NLP up in a nutshell.

The easiest way to understand NLP is to break down the N, L and P :

- **Neuro** is the use of our senses to filter and process our experiences.
  We see, hear, feel, taste and smell our own version of reality.
- **Linguistic** is the language we use to express our interpretation of reality.
- **Programming** is the patterns of behaviour and thinking that we follow as a result of our filtering and processing of experiences.
  These patterns create structure to our experiences from which we communicate.

Once we recognise our own structures and patterns we can change them to influence our outcomes.

Similarly when we understand structures and patterns of others we can influence and support them, thereby creating a world of possibilities.

In summary, NLP is devoted to learning how to think and communicate with yourself and others more effectively.

The Model

The core principles or pillars of NLP are:

- **Rapport** – this is about relationship with yourself.
  It's about having congruence and integrity whereby the whole of you is in alignment.
  It's about relationships with others in order to effectively influence and achieve what you really want.
- **Sensory Awareness** – this is the "neuro" of neuro linguistic programming which means using your senses - looking at, listening to and feeling what is happening to you and others.
- **Outcome Thinking** – this is establishing exactly what you want.
  This could be what you want in any given situation or a larger life outcome.
- **Behavioural Flexibility** – this is about using choice to do or think differently when what you currently do is not working.
  This is essential in achieving your outcome.

Pillars of NLP

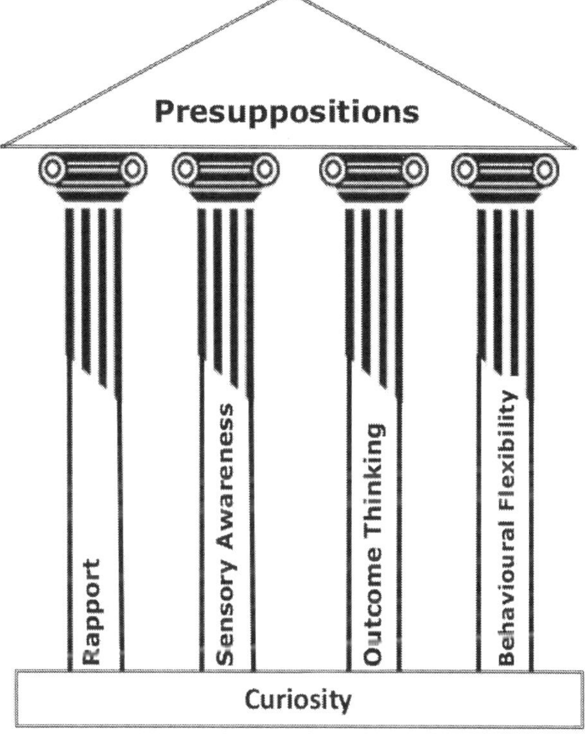

- **Curiosity** – this forms the foundations of the model.

  It is about accepting that you don't know all the answers but you are willing to use curiosity to investigate and understand what is happening within each of the four pillars.

  It is about questioning and noticing what you notice.

- **Presuppositions** – these are about freeing the beliefs and values that you hold.
  In conjunction with a non-judgmental curiosity, presuppositions can expand learning and awareness.

Why is NLP useful?

Imagine having the skills to know what it is you really want and you have all of the communication, awareness and flexibility to achieve it every time.

From the Model derives a multitude of tools and techniques that can be utilised to give you exactly that.

These tools and techniques become a way of life in your personal and professional environments and will help you establish and achieve your goals and directions.

As an Executive PA NLP provides you with an awareness of how you "tick" and how others "tick" – particularly the people you support in your role.

With NLP skills and awareness you can be flexible in your thinking and behaviour in order to get the response or reaction that you need.

You will have the skills to create deep rapport with those around you, to better understand where a person is "coming from".

The 'N' Pearl:

> **"You have brains in your head.**
> **You have feet in your shoes.**
> **You can steer yourself any direction you choose."**
> **Dr Seuss**

"Now this is how it feels"   Few Peeps©

O is for Opinionated

O is for...Opinionated

Opinionated? That's a matter of opinion!

Putting forward your Opinion with Impact

When you feel very strongly about something it can be easy to let your emotions get the better of you and by doing so you can lose or dilute the impact of sharing your opinion.

There's an art to putting forward and sharing your opinion in a way that "lands" with the best impact . Notice I've used the word "share" here – this is about sharing your opinion not enforcing your opinion on someone else – it's about respecting the fact that not everyone will have the same opinion as you.

The following guidelines will help you put forward your opinion with impact.

1. Breathe! When you feel strongly about something this may show in your fast-paced breathing, body language and pace of talking. You need to get the balance right here between sharing your opinion with "passion" without appearing flustered, harassed or "bulldozing". By focusing on maintaining even, steady breathing this will help enormously.

2. Ground yourself and be assertive! Plant your feet firmly on the ground and ensure your body language is assertive – so match the level of someone else (if they are standing, you

stand, if they are sitting, you sit). Open the palms of your hands and maintain a steady, gentle eye-contact with the person you are talking to. Your tone of voice needs to be assertive too with an even paced steady rhythm that emphasises the important words or phrases at a volume that is audible to your audience (without shouting). *You can read more about assertiveness in the A is for Assertiveness Pearl of Wisdom.*

3. Favour Curiosity over Judgment. Human nature is such that we tend to "pre-judge" others based on our own experience and beliefs – put aside any prejudgments you make and instead be curious. Curiosity is the foundation to all learning and opens our mind to ensure we are more receptive and aware in any situation.

4. Acknowledge someone else's opinion. Not everyone will have the same opinion as you. We are all unique human beings with individual experiences, beliefs, upbringing, knowledge and learning. Acknowledge that someone else may have a different opinion to you, e.g. "I understand you have/may have a different opinion here and I'm sure, like me, you appreciate that we're all different."

5. Seal it with a KISS! (Keep It Short & Simple). Cut through any jargon by using simple language that can be instantly understood. *You can read more about this in the K is for KISS Pearl of Wisdom.*

6. Explain your reasons for having the opinion that you do: e.g. "This is my opinion because in my experience x has happened...." or "I'm basing my opinion on ....."

7. Tailor your language to suit the person you are delivering your message to - learn about VAK systems. Did you know that, whilst we access all five senses to "make sense" of our worlds, in fact most of us have a dominant or primary sense that we use over the others? And the language and favoured vocabulary that we use relates directly to that primary sense. Talking someone else's language means you are more easily able to create rapport with them and have a "connection" – crucial if you want to deliver your message with real impact. *You can read more about this in the C is for Communication Pearl of Wisdom.*
    As we've seen, Nelson Mandela said *"if you talk to a man in a language he understands that goes to his head. If you talk to him in his language, that goes to his heart".* In order to create deep rapport and deliver your message with real impact, you want to be able to use another person's preferred language set.

8. Be open to hearing someone else's opinion. Someone else has given you their time to listen to your opinion – which you've delivered with impact. Reciprocate by giving them time to share theirs.

The 'O' Pearl:

> ***"Tact is the art of making a point without making an enemy"***
> ***Isaac Newton***

"Snapping the snapper"   Few Peeps©

P is for Perceptual Positions

P is for... Perceptual Positions (step into my shoes...)

"The person with the most flexibility in thinking and behaviour has the most influence over any situation"

How often have you been in a situation and found yourself confused or frustrated at the response or behaviour of someone else?

How often have you asked yourself - *"why have they acted in such a defensive / negative / destructive / inappropriate way?"*

In situations where you are faced with confusion and frustration at someone else's attitude, behaviour or actions, what can you do?

Well, firstly you can have Curiosity, something I consider to be the foundation to all learning.

You need to have the curiosity to find out the reasons behind someone eliciting a particular behaviour or responded in the way that they have.

Because, without curiosity you can lose sight of what your original outcome for a situation is.

Then you can put into practice the technique known as "perceptual positions", which allows you to gain insight into a situation by looking at it and considering it from three different perspectives.

First Position (your own)

"Wearing your own shoes" and fully experiencing what is important to you. This is known as being "associated" into your experience.

Second Position (the other person's)

By "wearing their shoes" and being fully associated with what is important to them.

Third Position (from the outside)

By taking a disassociated and analytical view of what is happening between 1 and 2.

By gaining this insight we give ourselves choices and flexibility about the actions we can take in order to support our outcomes.

Here is the Technique:-

1. From first position and "in your own shoes" think about the situation from your point of view.
2. Ask yourself:
   What is important to me?
   How does this affect me?
   What is my desired outcome from this situation?
   Take a mental note of these.
3. From second position and stepping into "the other person's shoes", think about what is important to them.
4. See, hear and feel the world from their position.
5. Take on the other person's physiology and think about their beliefs and values, what do you already

know about this person that will help you understand it from their perspective?

This will allow you to become fully associated into their world.

6. From third position and like "a fly on the wall", you move to the position of an independent eye-witness.

   You observe and comment on the facts of the situation without feeling or emotion.

   You can therefore give yourself disassociated advice on what would be useful in order to improve the situation and gain a better understanding of what is going on.

A good way to work with this technique is to physically move between positions to experience the different perspectives.

Position two chairs - sit on one to experience first position then move to the other chair to experience second position. Stand back to experience third position from a distance.

Think about what happens when someone becomes "stuck" in any of the three positions too.

- A person stuck in first position can become selfish and egotistical.
- In second position the person can be over-influenced and co-dependent on the views of those around them.
- In third position a person can become emotionally-detached and unfeeling.

With the flexibility to move (physically and in your mind and thinking) you will find this technique beneficial to increase your awareness during a given situation.

And, of course, the person with the most flexibility in thinking and behaviour, has the most influence over any situation.

Perceptual Positions

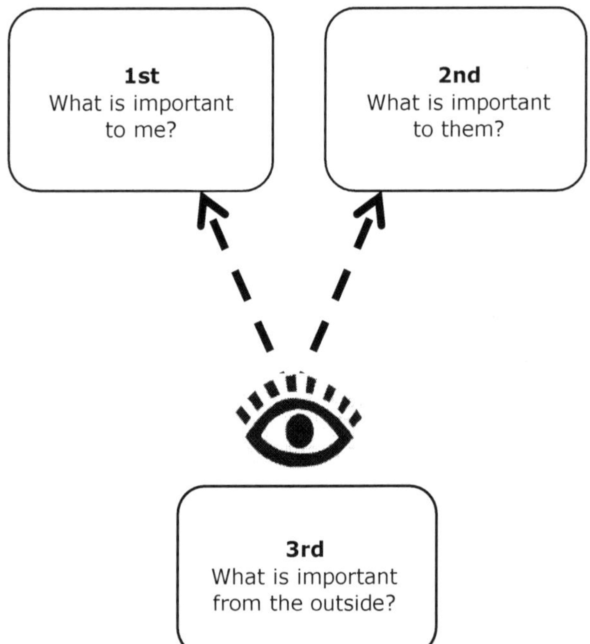

The 'P' Pearl:

> **"Sometimes we need to take a different perspective to see things clearly"**
> **Nick Fewings**

"Where are we?"   Few Peeps©

Q is for Quality Questions

Q is for...Quality Questions

"A Quality Question is made up of asking the right person the right question in the right way" Lindsay Taylor

Quality Questions give quality responses and answers. They provide you with the information you need or want quickly and efficiently. Ensuring you get it right first time will save you time and energy and will ensure your credibility in the workplace as a highly organised and time-efficient PA.

Firstly, ensure you are clear about the information you need or want and identify the best (and therefore right) person to get this information from.

What do you know about this person with regard to how they like to communicate (think about VAK systems and read the C is for Communication Pearl of Wisdom)?

Asking your question in the right way using a combination of their preferred language will ensure great rapport between you – and therefore a better likelihood of getting the very best (and highest quality) response.

Also think about whether it is going to be best / quicker to get the response you need by asking the question of someone face to face (or over the phone) or by sending the question via email?

Identify the right question to ask. Do you need to ask an "open question" to facilitate lots of information? Or do you need to clarify information or a request of you by asking a closed question (one that invites a yes or no response)?

I have a favourite open questions model that I introduce to PA clients (and one that raises a lot of giggling from my young daughter!). This is the "5 bottoms on a rugby post" model.

Transpose the word "bottoms" for "derrieres" or "behinds" – whichever you prefer - and I challenge you not to giggle like my daughter!

Imagine some rugby posts (the letter "H" for our "How" questions) and on the crossbar of the rugby posts imagine 5 rugby bottoms (or "W's" for our "W" questions – namely, What, Why, Where, Who, When).

You will notice that the "Why" question in the model has a warning triangle by it – the reason? Because asking a "why" question can be received in an accusatory way and therefore the response you get may be a defensive one.

Also, as a questioner you can find yourself in a "why" spiral, asking a quick succession of "why" questions whilst never quite getting the highest quality response.

Rephrasing your question to "what's important…." or "what's important about…." ensures you are getting to the real "crux" of a matter, the heart of the question and ensuring a quality response that has invited the respondent to think deeply about the question posed to them.

Open Questions

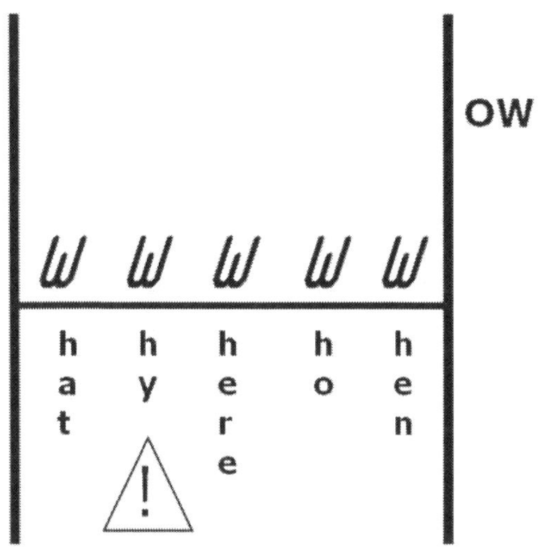

The 'Q' Pearl:

> *"The art and science of asking questions is the source of all knowledge"*
> *Thomas Berger*

"Ready for the off"   Few Peeps©

R is for Red lorry, yellow lorry

R is for... Red lorry, yellow lorry

As a busy PA and Executive Assistant having to "think on your feet" is part and parcel of your role – you need to work quickly and efficiently without getting tongue-tied – in order to foster credibility and respect in your workplace.

So, how do you achieve this?

1. **"Failing to plan is planning to fail"**

    Be as prepared as you can be for every eventuality.

    Pre-empt any impending or likely situations that could arise, holding the belief that "Failing to plan is planning to fail."

    An excellent PA is proactive and always at least one step ahead of the situation.

2. **Identify your outcome – what do you want or need to achieve?**

    Once you've identified any impending or likely situations, articulate your outcome and what it is you need or want to achieve.

    Use precise, towards language to verbalise this outcome.

Towards language is vocabulary that has momentum and forward movement – you are moving towards achieving, gaining and getting the outcome you want.

Use the following format: [In the event that xxx happens, I will xxx.]

3. **See, hear and feel it!**

Rehearse the situation in your mind.

Metaphorically step forward in time and imagine you have achieved your outcome.

Notice what you can see, notice what you can hear yourself and others saying, and notice how you feel.

In effect you are creating a sensory rich "future memory" – and, as sensory rich beings, that's a powerful thing to do.

This is a technique called "creative visualisation" and is something used by successful leaders across the world.

Remember the "I is for Imagination" Pearl of Wisdom you read?

4. **Fact find**

Gain as much information upfront as you can for the impending or likely situations you have identified.

- What would you continue doing?

- What would you stop doing?

- What would you start doing? "

The 'R' Pearl:

> *"Want to go really fast?*
> *Slow down and focus"*
> *Tim Fargo*

"I don't need these"   Few Peeps©

S is for Something to be learned from every situation

S is for... Something to be learned from every situation

or

'Tapping in to different environments'

Whilst visiting the ladies room of a (rather nice!) restaurant in London one week, a little incident got me to thinking...

I was stood at the washbasins next to another lady and we were both struggling to work out how to "turn" the tap on (or for those of you reading in the States... the faucet).

The other lady tried pushing the top of the tap.

I tried turning it.

Neither of us was correct. It was a lift top.

The other lady turned the tap right to make the water warmer.

I turned it left.

The other lady was correct.

We looked up at our reflections in the mirror above the wash basins and laughed together - remarking in stereo "taps are so challenging nowadays!".

Long gone are the original turn taps with one for hot and one for cold, clearly marked with "H" and "C" – now there are many different variations of taps and ways to operate them.

And this fact and little incident got me to thinking about what we can learn and transpose to our work environments with their ever changing and developing technology and initiatives:

Never assume anything

As human beings we tend to "prejudge" situations based on our previous experience and knowledge – this can limit our thinking and mean we miss out on opportunities that could be "staring us right in the face".

By being curious and approaching every new environment or situation with an open and inquisitive mind you are opening up more possibilities.

Be prepared

When faced with a new environment or situation ensure you have prepared yourself as much as possible.

Follow the adage "Failing to plan is planning to fail".

Be clear about what it is you want to achieve

For every situation you find yourself in it is really important to know what it is you want (or need) to achieve.

Then think about how you are going to achieve it - what action do you need to take to ensure things work and flow?

Relating this to the tap analogy:

Do you need to twist the tap, turn the tap or lift up the tap?

How much strength do you need to exert to ensure things flow and work as you want or need them to?

Ask yourself some great questions!

What do you already know about the new environment or situation?

How can you find out more?

Who would be able to help you?

What things (or people) are you going to need with you?

How do YOU need to be (for example focused, motivated, assertive, confident)?

"If at first you don't succeed, try, try again"

Determination and staying power are key .

Hindsight is a great thing – so, if things don't work out as you had hoped the first time around, learn from your experience.

Give yourself some feedback by asking next time around,

-        What will I do differently?

- What will I stop doing?

- What will I start doing?

- What will I continue doing?

And remember - there is no failure – only feedback!

Act your shoe size not your age....

The average shoe size for UK women is a size 6. I have knowledge of 6 years olds as a mum to a son (now 17) and daughter (now 10) so I've "been there". Twice. Plus I studied child psychology and I'm a trained nursery nurse. I want to introduce to you that acting your shoe size not your age has huge benefits for you on your learning journey.

In a society where our schools and parenting styles value individualism and "every child matters", I appreciate that there is no one "normal", cookie-cutter and stereotypical 6 year old. Just like there is no one "normal", cookie-cutter and stereotypical Executive PA. I repeat – I have experience of 6 years old and I know that my 6 year old son was a very different character to my 6 year old daughter. We're all unique and that's something I truly value – diversity and the excitement of different personalities and characters in our lives. For the most part however and as a basis for our learning here, a child of 6 will demonstrate characteristics and behaviours synonymous with theoretical understanding from some of our much revered and quoted experts and psychoanalysts. One such psychoanalyst is German-born Erik Erikson (1902 -1994) famed for his theory on psychosocial development in humans and a former Professor at American Universities Yale and Harvard.

It is those characteristics of a 6 year old identified by Erikson that I want to unpick. I want to emphasise that these characteristics and behaviours are things we can tap into as adults (based on the very knowledge that we now have as adults). I am going to highlight the advantages of "acting your shoe size and not your age" to aid our own learning, development and ultimate success.   By "stepping in" to your 6 year old self again you can approach learning with a renewed, regenerated enthusiasm and love of learning.

So, what is Erikson's theory on a child of 6?

According to Erikson as a child of 6 you enter the stage of "Competence". You pick up a multitude of new skills, learning and competencies and thus develop a "sense of industry". You have the desire and the enthusiasm to want to learn. Positive reinforcement is essential to you at this stage in order to promote your own self esteem.

As a specialist trainer of PAs and Administrative Professionals across the world, I am (of course) am advocate of life-long learning and believe every opportunity is a learning experience   We are picking up new knowledge and skills every day of our lives – sometimes without realising it.

Take just a few minutes at the end of the day, every day, and ask yourself "what have I learned today?", "what can I do with this new knowledge or with this new skill to benefit me and those around me?".

Take ownership of your own skills and learning achievements. If you could go back to your 6 year old self and give yourself some advice on the skills and learning that would be really useful to pick up for your older self – what would they be?   It is never, ever too late to pick up a new skill and if you've identified something on answering that question that you would like to have now– how can you go about gaining it? Who do you know that can help you gain that skill or learning? What has held you back in the past (or is holding you back now) from gaining that skill? How can you overcome this obstacle or barrier? What is the first step you can take in ensuring you can, and indeed will, gain this skill?

Your 6 year old self had a love for learning and picking up new skills and information – imagine that enthusiasm now for you, as an adult learner – "step" in to being 6 again to ensure you approach every new learning experience with curiosity and energy. Imagine having that real enthusiasm for learning that you had at age 6.

Erikson believed that at age 6 positive reinforcement was a major factor in building our self-esteem. It is true to say that positive reinforcement is a motivator to us all. Admittedly some rely more heavily on feedback from an external source than others – but ultimately that pat on the back, that affirmation that you're doing a good job is a big boost to you and your ultimate success. If that's something you're not getting at your current workplace – go out of your way to get it. Have the conversation with your peers and let them know that for you to be motivated you would appreciate and value their feedback on how you're doing. And remember, the highest quality feedback is given for your personal development and effectiveness. As a 6 year old you thrive on knowing you are doing a great job – it boosts your self-esteem – the same can be applied to you, as an adult learner, now.

The Competence Learning Ladder

I'm going to share with you a really useful model around competence which acts as a simple and very helpful explanation of how we learn. Essentially we work our way up a ladder of learning from Unconscious Incompetence to the top rung of Unconscious Competence.

- _Unconscious Incompetence_

  You are not aware of the existence or indeed relevance of the skill or learning. Before any development can happen you need to be conscious of the skill. Trainers and teachers play an essential role here in helping you identify a deficiency in your skillset and making you aware of the benefit to your personal effectiveness in gaining that skill or learning.

- _Conscious Incompetence_

  You become aware of the relevance and benefit to you of the skill or learning and ideally embrace the need and want to gain this skill in order to improve your effectiveness. Having a clear idea of the extent of the deficiency and what level of skill is required is essential for you to move to the Conscious Competence stage – as is your commitment to learn and practice the new skill.

- _Conscious Competence_

  This is when you can successfully and personally perform a skill without assistance - but still have to concentrate on applying it – it is not yet "second nature".   "Practice makes perfect" applies perfectly here if you are to make the move to Unconscious Competence.

•   <u>*Unconscious Competence*</u>

This is when you become practiced at a skill so it is "second nature" – a good and common example is driving. Because the skill has become in effect more instinctual, you can perform that skill at the same time as doing something else – for example, you can hold a conversation whilst driving a car. A great friend and trainer of mine describes this as "in the muscle" – the skill you are performing has entered the unconscious part of your brain.

Importantly, now you are at the top rung of the Competence Ladder, it is essential to "not take things for granted" – very often we can become complacent here and fall in to bad habits or consider ourselves to be expert in a particular field, skill or learning to the determinant of ourselves and others.   To be at the very top of your effectiveness may necessitate you moving down a rung on the ladder and taking stock of your unconscious competencies.   Put into practice conscious competence and consciously concentrate on practicing the skill or learning.   Check in with yourself on your level of complacency and ask yourself how up to date your skills are too.

Understanding the competence ladder and "acting your shoe size and not your age" means you can harness the enthusiasm and the desire to learn. Ultimately you can take ownership of your own learning journey and ensure you learn something from every opportunity.

The 'S' Pearl:

> *"When the winds of change blow, some people build walls and others build windmills"*
> **Chinese Proverb**

"Waiting in Departures"   Few Peeps©

T is for Time

T is for... Time

If you have an assumption that I'm going to share with you all the skills of time management, you are mistaken. For, I feel this would be an imitation Pearl, regurgitating the learning that is already available to you. My recommendation to you for time management expertise is to read Stephen R Covey's "**7 Habits of Highly Effective People**". You'll gain some amazing insights in to those individuals who are the most personally effective and who can prioritise their workload in terms of urgency and importance.

What I'm going to share with you is more of a "Time Travel" Pearl based on a blog post I wrote for www.wearethecity.com – an amazing resource that I'm proud to support.

What would Granny say?

There was something very romantic and magical about travelling back in time with Granny. At the age of about ten I remember asking Granny to share stories of 'The Olden Days'. Stood in the tiny galley kitchen of her Berkshire home, Granny worked through the archives of her memories whilst dunking and poking the steaming washing in the twin tub with a long handled wooden spoon.

Washing days were a major operation at Granny's house - the twin tub was hauled in to position in the middle of the kitchen, the room filled with steam and the stories my Granny shared took on a dreamy quality in the resulting clouds of air that surrounded us.

One of the Bletchley code breakers, my Granny had a secretive smile when recalling the 'war years'. She shared stories of her fellow workers including an aristocratic Lady whose facial beauty was legendary but who was 'cursed with thick black hairs on her legs' (my granny's words not mine!). Granny re-lived evenings preparing for tea dances and grand balls where gravy browning was used to colour your legs and drawing a line of kohl down the back gave the illusion of wearing stockings, when large pots of petroleum jelly took pride of place on the dressing table and the jelly was worked on to your eyelashes in place of mascara .... And always, always my Granny would finish the stories with damp eyes – but not from the steam of the washing.

Recalling these memories now as an adult, I feel a connection across time with my Granny and an appreciation of the nostalgia she must have been feeling as she recalled those war days. She was highly intelligent (hence being at Bletchley Park) and had felt valued at that time in using her intelligence. But when the war ended, like many other females of the time, she slotted back in to society's expectation of her - a stay-at-home wife and mother, running a household, caring for her working husband and hauling the twin tub in to position on wash days with resulting damp eyes.

I wonder - if we could bring Granny back now, what would she think about the women who are leaders and role models in today's society?

What advice would this intelligent woman give to me, her granddaughter, as I juggle the demands of being a Director of my own company with the demands of being a wife, mum, sister, daughter, friend and colleague?

I can imagine her "leaning in" (http://bit.ly/1wdlFnc) to her Kindle, reading and embracing Bonnie Low-Kramen's reasons why women should help other women (http://bit.ly/1s98NvN).

I'm certain Granny would break through the "coding" of society's expectations of women that exist even today, and I'm certain her advice would echo the feedback I give to my female clients.

"The thing that is holding You back from being The Most Successful - is actually You" she would say. "You have so many opportunities to potentially take advantage of". Then she would scroll through her Twitter feed of motivational quotes and Retweet her favourite "Teach your daughter to worry less about fitting into glass slippers and more about shattering glass ceilings".

"Absolutely lean in" she would say "and realise that your self-belief is your Enigma".

The 'T' Pearl:

> *"Every second, every minute,*
> *every hour, every day is yours*
> *to shape your future.*
> *Only time will tell if you've*
> *used it wisely"*
> *Nick Fewings*

"Shoreline stretch"   Few Peeps©

U is for Understanding your power as a PA

U is for...Understanding your power as a PA

As a specialist PA coach and trainer, I meet and work with PAs from different industry sectors and organisations.

As a former PA myself I also have first-hand knowledge of the role and I appreciate the diversity of the job and the challenges you face.

As a fun exercise to "kick start" many of my training sessions my PA clients collate information in an A-Z format to answer the questions **"what are you involved in doing?"** and **"what skills and attributes are needed to be an excellent PA?"**.

I've been running this exercise for several years now and have a pretty extensive – and impressive - list!

It is a sad fact that many PAs underestimate the value of their positions– they don't appreciate or understand the power that they actually have in their roles.

For many of you, the barrier to your success as PA is – well – You.

Fostering and nurturing self-belief and gaining a greater understanding of yourself is at the foundation of all of my training sessions and the A-Z Collation exercise is just one way of helping a PA understand their power.

The A-Z exercise is very often the first opportunity PAs have had to spend quality thinking time really getting to grips with what the PA role is all about.

What is evident from the exercise is that the PA is working at a high level in the organisation, they need to be adept at communicating with Directors, Stakeholders, fellow team members and PAs, clients, customers and visitors. They are privy to lots of information with discretion, integrity and professionalism key when this information is confidential and not yet available to their fellow employees.

For many PAs the exercise is a "light bulb moment" for them, a realisation of the varied and diverse roles they perform and it highlights that they are crucial to the running of their organisations.

The exercise also demonstrates that the expectations of a PA in one organisation can differ greatly to that at another organisation. Indeed, a PAs role can be directly determined by the department or Director he or she is working with.

It is absolutely true that there is no "one size fits all" job specification because of the very nature of the role and I personally don't think we would be adding any value by pushing for a standardised job specification.

Our emphasis needs to be that each PA has a current job specification that absolutely articulates and clarifies what they are involved in doing and the PA has an open, honest communication with their Director to agree their job purpose – you must know what is "in" and what is "out" and what you can be working on that will add the most value for you, your Director and ultimately your organisation.

By doing so you can then maintain those work boundaries and ultimately push back and say "no" *(you can read more in the H is for Helpful Pearl of Wisdom)* to ensure your credibility and professionalism in the workplace.

The 'U' Pearl:

> *"A bird sitting on a tree is never afraid of the branch breaking, because her trust is not on the branch but on her own wings.*
> *Always believe in yourself"*
> *Anonymous*

"Are you listening to me?" Few Peeps©

V is for Voice

V is for... Voice

Consider your position as a PA as highly privileged. The very nature of your role means you are privy to lots of company information, information that can be sensitive and confidential in nature. Very often you are first "in the know" on business matters ahead of your team members. Your privileged position throws up challenges in the form of knowing when to impart and share information and when not to impart and share information. Discretion and professional integrity rank high on your list of essential skills.

It makes sense that with your privileged position and being "in the know" you are ideally placed and suited to share your opinion and to be a voice in your organisation.

But how do you ensure your voice is heard, and valued, in your workplace?

Ask away

Sharing your opinion is, in effect, providing feedback. The highest quality feedback is offered to the listener. Your very first step in being a voice and sharing your opinion needs to be the question "Is it okay if I share my opinion with you?".

This gets the attention of the person you are delivering your opinion to and their "okay" and "seal of approval" that you can now go ahead with voicing your opinion.

You can also add kudos and credibility to your opinion by reminding your listener that you are in a privileged position. Imagine you've been involved in a new company initiative that your manager has instigated. You've been in the privileged position of knowing what's going on in the managerial world and also "on the floor" in terms of team members putting the initiative in to practice.

You could add some choice words here like "I'm sure you appreciate I've been heavily involved in this project and have been able to observe things not only from your perspective as a manager but also in terms of the team who have implemented it – so it is okay if I share my opinion with you?".

Use the 7, 38, 55 rule

Remember Mehrabian's research introduced to you in the A is for Assertiveness Pearl of Wisdom.

You can have a wonderful "script" ready to share (that's your 7% words) but unless you pay attention to "how" you deliver your message, in the tone of voice you use (the 38%) and how you look when you deliver it (55%), those words will be diluted.

Make sure you use words, tone & body language to deliver the most impactful message.

Practice makes perfect

Practise your message. Ask a friend or a colleague to help you out by pretending to be the person you are going to deliver your message to. Ask your friend for feedback – how well did your opinion come across? Did you use words, tone and body language to full effect? Could you add anything to make it more impactful?

If your message is of a sensitive nature and you can't practice with a friend or colleague, deliver your message in front of a full length mirror and give yourself feedback – remembering that the very best feedback is open and honest. *You can read more on Feedback to Self by reading Pearl of Wisdom F is for Feedback to Self.*

Be Empathetic

Remember, not everyone will have the same opinion as you – that's what makes the world (and the workplace) such an exciting place to be. That's what makes the world (and the workplace) such a challenging place to be! *You can read more about Empathy on Pearl of Wisdom E is for Empathy.*

The 'V' Pearl:

> *"Words mean more than what is set down on paper. It takes the human voice to infuse them with deeper meaning."*
> *Maya Angelou*

Few Peeps©

"Sole food, food for the soul"

W is for Wellbeing

W is for... Wellbeing

I am delighted to be sharing this Pearl of Wisdom written by our Wellness Associate at Your Excellency Ltd – Louise Lloyd.

Louise and I have worked together now for several years and I admire and respect her insightfulness and passion. Together we offer a specialist one day workshop for PAs and Admin Professionals.

Wellbeing for the PA

The role of the PA requires a diverse skill set to be implemented – very often at spinning "Wonder Woman" speed (and I mean no offence or discrimination to the male Pas out there – please transpose the words "Wonder Woman" for whatever super hero you favour!).

Similar to the grace of a swan serenely gliding across a lake, the PA is required to show effortless efficiency even when the underwater driving energy is operating at maximum capacity (and, let's be honest, often tangled with weeds!)

There is an expectation that the PA will ensure their Manager(s) glides across the water of their hectic schedules with the same swan like grace.

Of course in reality it rarely feels this smooth and whilst the PA does everything in their power to ensure both the efficiency and wellbeing of their Manager(s), looking after their own energy and wellbeing can be something of a challenge.

The PA comes in to contact with a great many different people aside from their Manager(s) – other team members, stakeholders, customers, clients and external suppliers to name but a few.

Developing emotional resilience is an absolute must for the PA to remain centred and balanced in their own energy whilst dealing with the varying emotional and mental states of all the other people they interact with in any given week.

The job also requires the PA to have the inner stability and mental flexibility to be able to adapt and change planned schedules at the drop of a hat, to come up with all the accurate documentation required for that changed schedule and to be able to operate under frequent interruption.

To say that multi-tasking and effective time management are crucial is an understatement then.

The PA spends most of their working life looking after and helping others and seem to have a genuine desire to strive to deliver often near impossible tasks however stretched they might already be.

In recognition of this effort, and in an attempt to make the PA's life a little easier here are my Top 10 Wellbeing Tips that will help to take that swan like effortless grace to the very core of your being.

1. Start every single day as a whole new day, and at the end of every day feel a sense of contentment

knowing that you have given that day your very best.

2. Learn to become more aware of the way that you are breathing.

When we are stressed or extremely busy we often fail to breathe well, causing tiredness and adding to stress and tension. As often as you can throughout the day take a single deep breath, and remind yourself that within that breath you have all the space and time that you need.

3. Learn to become more aware of your posture.

Our body is designed to be in an energy efficient posture that places the least amount of strain possible on the musculoskeletal system. Poor posture uses up unnecessary energy as well as potential physical discomfort developing.

Keep your shoulders back and down, your spine in a neutral position and try not to cross your legs when seated but rather keep your feet hip width apart on the floor.

When walking about keep your head held high - you will be amazed how much this can lift your energy levels and mood.

4. Learn to manage your time efficiently, and if you are a procrastinator try to understand your reasons for procrastinating and get that sorted out - procrastinating is a massive drain on our energy and obviously eats away at precious time.

5. Don't keep things in that might be worrying you or causing you stress.

Take the time to talk to someone else to get any problems resolved as soon as possible.

Churning unresolved problems over in our mind takes mind energy away from the tasks we need it for. A clear mind is an efficient mind.

6. Take regular breaks - however brief, and however busy you are.
    It is proven that people that take regular breaks are more efficient. A fresh mind is less likely to make mistakes.
7. There is plenty of information out there on healthy diets and we often feel like we are being told off for eating the wrong things, but it really is important to have a balanced healthy diet that works for you. The Wonder Woman (super-hero) PA needs the right fuel to keep energy levels high through the day and calm enough to ease into a good night's sleep to replenish the mind and body ready for the next day.
8. Keep hydrated. By the time you are thirsty you are already dehydrated and your efficiency levels will have dropped so sip plenty of water throughout each day and avoid fizzy, sugary drinks and too much caffeine.
9. Pay attention to any warning signs and get the help you need.
    If you do start to notice that you are feeling increasingly stressed or out of sorts then take a step back and get the help that you need. Life has its ups and downs and sometimes we all need a little extra help to keep us healthy and happy.
    Likewise, the body has an amazing way of telling us when we are out of balance emotionally and / or mentally so don't be too quick to take a pill or two to get rid of any physical symptoms before you have looked at why you might be getting them.
10. Make sure your life has room for fun.
    A good dose of laughter and a change of scene does us the world of good so remember life is here to be lived.

Keeping all things in perspective can help us to stop wasting energy worrying about things that don't really matter and free up energy for us to use on loving each other and loving life!

The 'W' Pearl:

> *"A day without laughter is a day wasted."*
> Charlie Chaplin

Few Peeps©

X is for X Marks The Spot

X is for...X marks the spot – how to uncover your personal treasure

In my work as a personal coach I help individuals identify what's important to them – what motivates them, what puts a smile on their face and what gives them that sense of satisfaction.

In essence I like to think about this as helping individuals identify their "map of the world" marked-up with the all-important "X" as a marker for uncovering personal treasure.

I believe that very often we fail to include time in our busy schedules for "quality thinking time".

We may feel that we need to be physically active and physically moving to be "achieving".

However, without quality thinking time – we could be moving in the wrong direction.

When our minds are active rather than our bodies, when we set aside time for quality-thinking and answering thought-provoking questions, we can identify what is important to us, where we are, where we are going and how we are going to get there.

And the knock-on effect of this quality thinking time is that our physical movement is more likely to be in the right direction, the best direction for us personally and we can ensure we are involved in activities that meet what is important to us.

We can identify our own treasure map marked-up with the all-important X that signifies our own personal treasure.

Consider the number of hours you spend in your work environment – you need to be "getting" all the things that are important to you in order to be the happiest, most satisfied and motivated.

So, our first step is identifying what those things actually are.

Set aside some quality thinking time for yourself and put in to practice this useful exercise which I shared with a recent coaching client.

I met with a coaching client the other week who has recently started a new position as a Private PA to a HNWI (High Net Worth Individual) –when they secured the role they were incredibly excited about it.

However, two months in to that role, they contacted me because they felt "something was missing" and wanted to identify what that "something" was.

We spent 30 minutes of quality thinking time.

I asked my client, if they could write an ideal job advert, what would it include?

My client identified the following in their ideal job advert

1	An opportunity to be creative (writing articles, blog posts)
2	A friendly, team environment

3	Opportunities to pull together PowerPoint presentations
4	Booking complex travel itineraries

We numbered these "criteria" and then I asked my client to compare them as follows, giving one "point" for the criteria that was most important in each case

- Compare 1 to 2, 1 to 3, 1 to 4
- Compare 2 to 3 and 2 to 4
- Compare 3 to 4.

We ended up with points assigned as follows:

1	An opportunity to be creative (writing articles, blog posts)	1	(1 point)
2	A friendly, team environment	111	(3 points)
3	Opportunities to pull together PowerPoint presentations		(0 points)
4	Booking complex travel itineraries	11	(2 points)

So in order of criteria and what was important to my client, their own personal treasure is:

2	A friendly, team environment	3 points
4	Booking complex travel itineraries	2 points

1	An opportunity to be creative (writing articles, blog posts)	1 point
3	Opportunities to pull together PowerPoint presentations	0 points

Now I asked my client in their current role working for the HNWI whether these things were being "met".

Whilst being involved in complex travel itineraries, writing articles and pulling together PowerPoint presentations, the "friendly, team environment" – at the very top of the criteria – was not being met.

The position involved the PA working from the individuals private home office, very often alone (as the HNWI was away on the very well organised complex travel itineraries!).

The most important of my PA client's personal treasure was not being met in her current role – the "something" that was missing for her being the most happy, satisfied and motivated had been identified.

Had my client conducted this exercise prior to securing her current job role she may have thought more carefully about accepting a positon that did not meet with her criteria, that did not give her the personal treasures she needs.

And for those of you who want to know the latest on my client, she had an open, honest conversation with the HNWI and shared with him that she needed a different working environment to be happy – they parted on good terms and just this morning she called me to say she had accepted a new position as a PA to the Marketing Director at a magazine publishers in London – working in a small, friendly office environment.

The 'X' Pearl:

> *"What did you do as a child that made the hours pass like minutes?*
> *Herein lies the key to your earthly pursuits"*
> *Carl Jung*

"Reflection Time"   Few Peeps©

Y is for You

Y is for... You!

Many of the Pearls of Wisdom in this book have introduced you to techniques, tools, models (call them what you will) which you can put into practice to be the very best you can be, so that you can achieve excellence in whatever you do.

One resounding message is that PAs need to be adaptable and flexible in their working styles.

As PAs we need an awareness of how we and others "tick".

We need to tailor how we work to suit our managers and our team, to ensure we get the very best out of ourselves and others.

I do feel I should put a "health warning" on this book though – for my intention is not to produce a robotic production line of cloned PAs.

This de-humanisation of you as individuals is not the purpose of sharing these Pearls of Wisdom

As I type this, I am all too aware of the journalistic scare-mongering rearing its head in the form of articles that tell us our profession will be redundant.

As technology advances, we are told the work we do can be replaced by robots, AI and apps (and of course, it can be done more efficiently negating the human-errors that inevitably do occur).

I abhorrently do not believe this.

For relationships are at the heart of any successful organisation and human contact will never be replaced by insensitive and characterless apps and robots.

Right at the very beginning of this book I acknowledged that the role of the PA is challenging and demanding – you are very often working with different (strong) characters in your organisations – this is what makes the workplace (and the world!) so challenging.

It is also what makes the workplace so exciting.

We are all unique.

We need to value this diversity.

My message to you is that, with all the great knowledge gleaned from these Pearls of Wisdom, you put them into practice but ensure you do not lose You.

A self-confident boost for You –

The PAS Model

Think about PAS as an acronym for

     Personality
     Attributes and
     Successes.

A great exercise to boost your self-confidence is to identify your top 3 Personality traits, your top 3 Attributes and your top 3 Successes.

Make a note of these.

You can also apply the PAS model to identify your weaknesses and areas that you want or need to work on to progress in your career.

Remember the very best feedback is open, honest feedback!

The 'Y' Pearl:

> *"Today you are You, that is truer than true.*
> *There is no one alive who is Youer than You."*
> *Dr Seuss*

"About to spring into action"   Few Peeps©

Z is for Zealous

Z is for... Zealous!

Okay, I admit it. Finding a word that began with Z that fitted with us as PAs was a little challenging - I toyed with the idea of writing about zzzzzz's and getting enough sleep in our profession (based on a rather interesting Facebook post that is doing the rounds on how much sleep children should be getting!) but then decided on Zealous because (she says, flicking though her Roget's Thesaurus – the old fashioned way......) it means

> Devoted   Diligent
>
> Dedicated   Enthusiastic
>
> Eager   and   Passionate

and I can imagine you all nodding now in agreement with those words being synonymous with the PA profession!

In fact the word "Zealous" appears on my A-Z collation document of the Executive PA. Just when I think I have a "complete" list I meet and work with another PA client who adds their own words and input!

So, I want to end this book with that collation sheet. I would so love to see you all reading this and nodding your heads in agreement at this true reflection of The Executive PA!

	What is the role of the Executive PA? What are you involved in doing?	What are the skills & attributes of the Executive PA?
A	Agendas Answering the phone Assisting & Supporting management in achieving their objectives Ambassador for your organisation Ambassador for the PA profession	Assertiveness Asks great questions Able to work with different personalities / deal with different people Adaptable Approach Articulate Amiable Awareness of manager's objectives, company's objectives + own objectives! Awareness of the industry in which you work
B	Booking hotels / meeting rooms Business Planning Budgets Bank Statements / Reconciliations Board Meetings	Build or develop someone else's ideas Being a "buffer" (gatekeeper) Bonding Building the team

	What is the role of the Executive PA? What are you involved in doing?	What are the skills & attributes of the Executive PA?
C	Communicating effectively with people at all levels, internally and externally Co-ordinating – whereabouts, time management of team, resources Catering Colleague Interaction Committee Meetings Customer / Client facing & liaison Controlling Coaching	Concentrates on what "can" be done rather than what "can't" be done Clear about what you want – using "I" statements Co-operative Committed Commercial & business awareness Confidence (in own ability!) Coaching Courageous Collaborator Curious (the foundation to all learning)
D	Diary management Database management Distribution of mail Delegate tasks Documentation	Diligent Determine Priorities Deadlines Discreet Dos & Don'ts

	What is the role of the Executive PA? What are you involved in doing?	What are the skills & attributes of the Executive PA?
	Decision Maker Delivering Development	Decisive Dynamic Driven Due Diligence
E	Event management Effective planning Email Management Expenses Evaluate Educate Excel Spreadsheets	Effective communicator Enthusiastic Effective planner Engaged Engaging Eloquent Establishing needs & wants Empathy EI (Emotional Intelligence)
F	Filing Fact finding Filter information (gatekeeper)	Focus on what is relevant in a situation Flexible Forward thinking

	What is the role of the Executive PA? What are you involved in doing?	What are the skills & attributes of the Executive PA?
	Finance	Filter Fun Friendly Feedback – can give & receive
G	Gaining / getting information Gatekeeper Governance Good Practice Geographically aware Gifts Guests	Give & receive feedback Goal orientated Great at whatever you do!! Gatekeeper Grounded Generous
H	Hotel bookings Help team and organisation achieve objectives / aims effectively HR Hospitality	Honest Helps others express their feelings Helpful Happy Hands-on approach

	What is the role of the Executive PA? What are you involved in doing?	What are the skills & attributes of the Executive PA?
		Hardworking
I	Increasing the output of the team by effective planning, organising and controlling time and other resources Implement (and maintain) systems and procedures for managing daily workload and keeping track of tasks IT Interviews Invoices	Integrity In depth knowledge of the organisation (Vision & Mission Statements, ethos) Inventive Information Source Initiative Intuitive Interpersonal skills Intelligence Independent worker Ideas generator Inspirational Inspired IT literate

	What is the role of the Executive PA? What are you involved in doing?	What are the skills & attributes of the Executive PA?
J	Juggling the demands of more than one "boss"	Juggler! Jargon-buster Justifying Judging Joyful
K	Keeping management up to date with what's happening Keeper of the Peace	Knowledge of organisation & industry in which organisation operates Keen Kind Kinship KISS (Keep it Short & Simple)
L	Logging telephone calls Liaison officer Leading Line Management Learning & Development	Listening skills Lenient Logical Liaising Loyal

	What is the role of the Executive PA? What are you involved in doing?	What are the skills & attributes of the Executive PA?
	Logistics	Likeable Lateral Thinking LinkedIn user
M	Managing the time of your management team Maintaining good working practices Minutes of meetings Meeting organising Merging / Managing Diaries Mentoring	Maintain boundaries (can say "no") Motivated Methodical Mind-reading Mindful Meticulous Morse Code Reader!
N	Negotiating Note keeper Networking Notify	Negotiator Nice
O	Organising (meetings, conferences, workload….)	Open & Honest in communication

	What is the role of the Executive PA? What are you involved in doing?	What are the skills & attributes of the Executive PA?
	Ordering – stationery / stock / catering Outlook use	One Step Ahead Organised Observe Oral Communication
P	Providing information at the right time so managers can make better decisions more quickly Projecting a professional image of the team & the organisation Prioritisation Personal Brand Photocopying Proofreading Presentations (PowerPoint) Planning Project Management Purchase Orders	Puts forwards ideas as suggestions (breeds agreement) as opposed to putting forward ideas as statements! Prioritisation skills Proactive Positive Mental Attitude Patience Practical Professional Project Management Skills (PRINCE) PowerPoint Perceptual (Positions)

	What is the role of the Executive PA? What are you involved in doing?	What are the skills & attributes of the Executive PA?
	Problem Solving	
Q	Questioning Queries	Quality Questions & Answers Quiet (knows when to be)
R	Relieving the management team of routine & administrative tasks Running the office so that it functions as a comprehensive information and communication centre for the organisation and its clients Reporting Recruitment Regulations	Recognises people have different views / opinions Reliable Resilient Respectful Robust Resourceful Responsible Reactive
S	Shorthand / Speedwriting Strategy Supervision	Seeks ideas (which in itself breeds giving ideas)

What is the role of the Executive PA? What are you involved in doing?	What are the skills & attributes of the Executive PA?
Shredding Solving problems Supporting Teams Spreadsheets Stationery Study Slides Social Media	Supports or agrees with something someone else has said (as opposed to explicity disagreeing or pointing out the difficulties and snags) Seeks clarification or information Sense of humour Self-motivated Shares ideas and goals with manager(s) and team Structured Systematic Straight-talking Strategic thinking Strict Social Awareness Sensitivity Speed SMARTer goal setting

	What is the role of the Executive PA? What are you involved in doing?	What are the skills & attributes of the Executive PA?
T	Timely productive of tasks Typing up reports etc. Training Events Training Needs Travel Itineraries	Time Management Team member / team work Trustworthy Tactful Tenacious Together(ness) Twitter user
U	Understudy Undertaking duties in job remit / spec	Understanding of organisations objectives (and therefore manager's objectives) Understand management styles & motivation United
V	Visions & Values Visitor greeting Vacancies Video Conferencing Visio (Org Charts software package)	Voice (to be heard!) Verbal Vital to the team Versatile Vocal

	What is the role of the Executive PA? What are you involved in doing?	What are the skills & attributes of the Executive PA?
W	Workload Word (Office) Water	Works in partnership with their manager(s) Willing & Able Wise Well Formed Outcomes
X	Xeroxing! EXcellent Excel spreadsheets	Excel software use Excellent at whatever you do! Exceptional Communication Skills X-ray Vision
Y	Yearly Meetings and appointments	Yourself! Youthful
Z		Zealous Zookeeper Zero Errors Zoned-in / Focused Zippy

And so we end our final pearl, the 'Z' Pearl:

> *"Life is not a dress rehearsal"*
> *Rose Tremain*

About the Author

Lindsay Taylor is the Director of Your Excellency Limited, an executive training and coaching organisation in the UK.

Lindsay specialises in delivering training and coaching to PAs, EAs, Secretaries and Administrators across the world and believes that fun, experiential training delivered in a jargon-free down-to-earth manner will ensure a memorable experience and optimise learning.

Lindsay herself spent 10 years as a PA and Executive Assistant in organisations in the UK and USA, including Transamerica Corporation the innovative financial services and products provider.

When Lindsay retrained as a Coach and Trainer, gaining practitioner status in Neuro Linguistic Programming, (NLP), she realised the huge benefit of these skills to PAs in improving and maintaining a great working relationship – with themselves, their boss and the teams they support.

Lindsay is passionate about sharing her knowledge. She develops and delivers unique programmes that utilise the tools and techniques of NLP in a fun, jargon-free way ensuring the skills are instantly useable by PAs to reach their full potential.

In the UK Lindsay is renowned for developing and delivering the fun and experiential workshop "Be a PA with PA – Perfect Awareness" specifically for PAs, EAs, Secretaries and Administrators. Lindsay believes the tools and techniques are hugely beneficial to PAs in improving and maintaining a good working relationship, enabling them to work more effectively and efficiently in supporting individuals, teams and the business as a whole.

The workshop receives high acclaim across the UK for providing communication, awareness and rapport-building skills to PAs serious about creating a strong professional identity and ensuring their time is spent as effectively and efficiently as possible. The training carries the endorsement of The IAM (Institute of Administrative Management).

Lindsay is an Associate Trainer and Consultant for a number of global learning and development providers. She develops and delivers bespoke programmes to administrators worldwide, something she readily admits is her favourite aspect of training as she believes travel is one of life's great educators.

Previous delegates and attendees of Lindsay's training have commented:

- *"Lindsay is a brilliant trainer - attentive, engaging and patient with the group, along with her wealth of*

PA experience which we could all relate to" PA to CEO (UK)

- *"It has been a delight to work with Lindsay. Our delegates benefitted greatly from her insights, knowledge and experience of the PA role"* Conference Producer *(Kuala Lumpur)*

- *"Lindsay is a highly supportive coach and trainer. Her workshops are relevant and extremely useful for any assistant who would like to gain awareness and communication techniques for their working and personal lives"* Award Winning PA, Charity Sector (UK)

- *"The energy & passion Lindsay has to deliver a great learning workshop is invaluable. The workshop enabled me to learn more about myself and how I come across to colleagues"* PA to CEO (UK)

- *"I had the pleasure of attending one of Lindsay's workshops in Dubai..... an enjoyable, interactive and fascinating experience. I have already been able to make use of what I learned. I would definitely recommend Lindsay and Your Excellency to give you a training experience that is out of the ordinary."* Office Manager, National Research Foundation (UAE)

- *"A must for all PA's or those working in a 'team' environment. Gives a greater understanding of what makes people tick"* President, Association of Celebrity Assistants (UK)

- *"Best workshop so far – real advice for real people – totally practical and fun"* PA, National Health Service (UK)

- *"One of the most interesting and informative course I have ever done!"* PA, Legal Firm, London (UK)

- *"Lindsay exudes friendly professionalism, teaching instantly useable skills in a down to earth manner"* PA, Private Estate (UK)

Lindsay grew up in Hong Kong and has lived in the UK, France and the US.

She adores the experience of working in different cultures and meeting new people.

She thrives on being busy – approaching everything she does with energy, drive and a real zest for life.

To contact Lindsay, please visit:

<u>www.yourexcellency.co.uk</u>

Lindsay is a fan of Twitter and can be followed on @Your_Excellency

Made in the USA
Columbia, SC
08 November 2017